A Photographic Record of Colonial Queensland

THE WORK OF JOHN HENRY MILLS

PROFESSIONAL PHOTOGRAPHER
1851 – 1919

Lyall Ford

Published by:
Taipan Press
PO Box 48
Freshwater
Queensland 4870
Australia

http://www.taipanpress.com.au

Ford, Lyall R.

A photographic record of colonial Queensland: the work of John Henry Mills: professional photographer: 1851 – 1919.

Bibliography.
ISBN 0 9590776 2 6

1. Mills, John Henry, 1851-1919. 2. Queensland - Pictorial works. I. Title.

919.43

Cover Photograph: The Reckitt & Mills Photographic Studio at Mount Britton, 1881

Printed by: Fergies, Brisbane, Queensland.

To my loving wife

Penelope (Penny)

About the Author

Lyall Ford is a Civil Engineer, Historian and Author. Born and raised in Mackay, he has lived and worked in several different towns in Central and North Queensland. He is married to Penelope (Penny) and they have four children, Miles, Felicity, Christopher and Stephanie.

Lyall has been researching Queensland history for decades and has taken a particular interest in the history of the Mackay district and the photography of John Henry Mills, his great grandfather.

In both 2002 and 2003, he received awards from the Queensland Family History Society for the best family history book published in Queensland, and in 2003, *Below These Mountains* was awarded third place by the Australian Institute of Genealogical Studies in Melbourne in the prestigious Alexander Henderson Awards for best family history published in Australia.

By the same author

Poorhouse to Paradise: The Adventures of a Pioneering Family in a North Queensland Country Town, Taipan Press, Cairns, 2001

Below These Mountains: The Adventures of John Henry Mills – Pioneer Photographer and Gold Miner, Taipan Press, Cairns, 2001

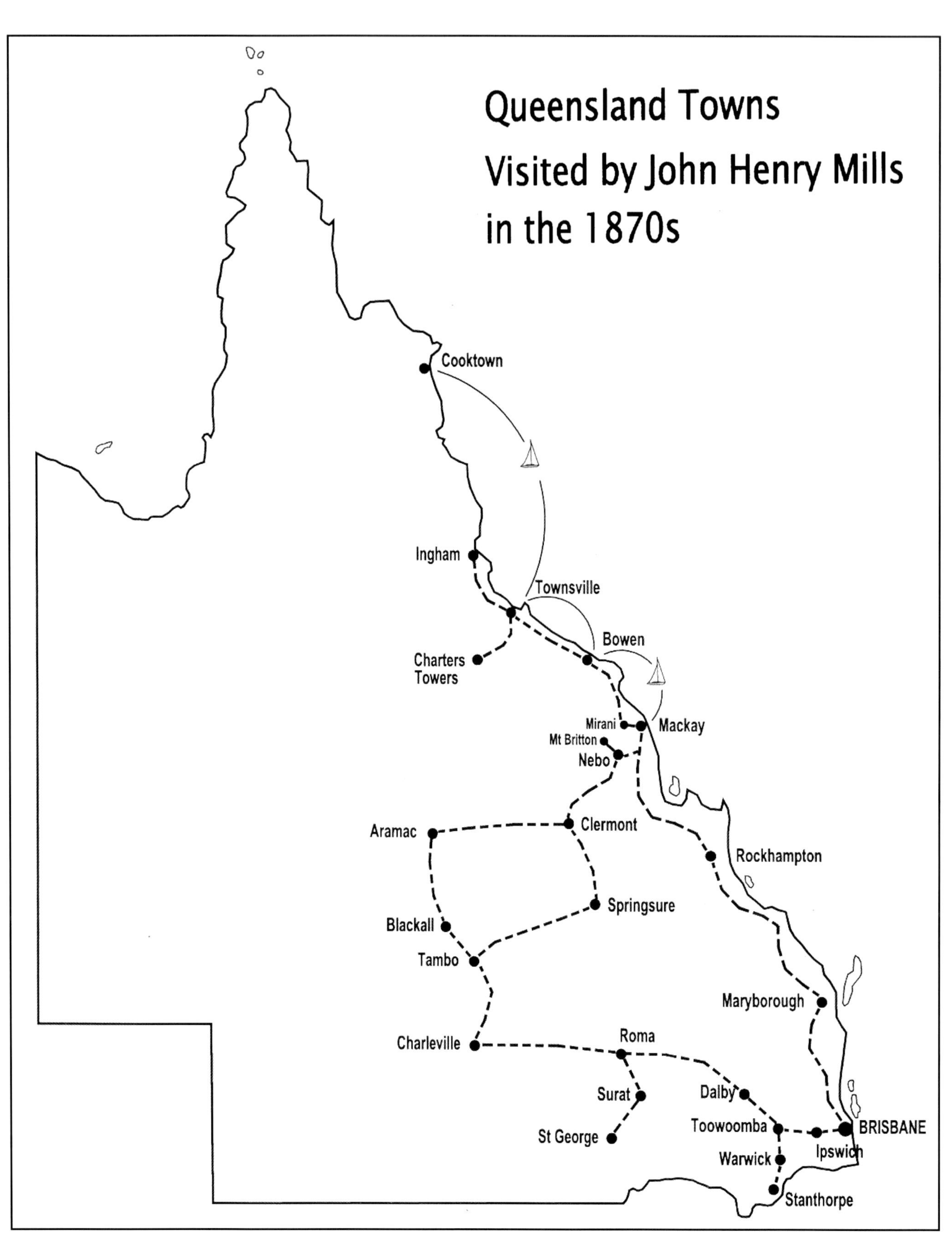
Queensland Towns
Visited by John Henry Mills
in the 1870s
Cooktown
Ingham
Townsville
Charters
Towers
Bowen
Mirani
Mackay
Mt Britton
Nebo
Clermont
Aramac
Rockhampton
Springsure
Blackall
Tambo
Maryborough
Charleville
Roma
Surat
Dalby
St George
Toowoomba
BRISBANE
Ipswich
Warwick
Stanthorpe

Contents

Foreword

Photographic images have become so much part of our lives that we barely notice them. They stare out at us from newspapers and magazines, books and street posters. We all have our own personal collections of family snaps, memorabilia of our lives, and most of us have owned a series of cameras of varying levels of sophistication, from Box Brownies to modern digital cameras. We take the existence of cameras for granted and there is no particular reason to think back to the origins of the process by which reality is captured on to light sensitive emulsion and metal, glass, paper or cellulose nitrate or cellulose acetate negatives. But the process is not really very old, and in its early decades it was a quite scientific art form. Cameras were on tripods, the lenses had to be set, the backdrop chosen, the sitters cajoled to remain still for a long period, and the end product had to be developed, cropped, tinted and enlarged. It was an expensive hobby for the rich and a profession for a few.

The wet plate process dates back to the 1830s, of which the Daguerreotype process invented in 1839 was the most successful. They were positive images on a metal support. The quality was exceptional but the process was cumbersome. Copper plates were exposed to iodine, the fumes forming light-sensitive silver iodine, and the plate had to be used within an hour. Exposures were for 10 to 20 minutes, during which time there could be no movement, and developing used heated mercury, a warm solution of salt and rinsing in hot distilled water. The invention of the dry plate process in 1878 meant that portable darkrooms were no longer necessary, the process was much more sensitive to light, and relatively fast shutter speeds were possible. Cameras became much more simple and portable, allowing more outside scenes to be captured. The final inventions late in the nineteenth century were film strips loaded as cartridges and cheaper cameras, basically the same process that has survived through until today. The photos taken by John Henry Mills and his partners involved all three processes, but were mainly dry plate productions. All are of wonderful quality.

In recent decades historians have become more conscious of the power of pictures. Photographs are fragments of the past and we need to be aware that they can be casual snaps or careful constructions, and that we can deconstruct the images in our analysis of years gone by. We are inclined to accept their reality and use them as factual evidence of what life was like long ago, but just as today, when we can easily reshape photographic evidence with the help of a personal computer, scanner and a Photoshop programme, professional photographers have always been able to alter images while locked away in the darkness of developing rooms with their chemical baths turning negatives into photographs. The Mills photos need to be 'read' both as a record and as careful constructions. Why did certain images interest him, and how did he create the shots? He was a commercial photographer, so his images had a particular purpose. Most of those reproduced here are general views, not just portraits of individuals, although we know that these were also a major part of his business. They illustrate both his travels in Queensland, and the places around which he lived.

The third element is the selection process for this book. Mills and his partners took thousands of photographs. Lyall Ford, one of John Henry Mills' descendants, has already produced two important books on his family, *Below These Mountains: the Adventures of John Henry Mills* (2001) and *Poorhouse to Paradise: The Adventures of a Pioneering Family in a North Queensland Country Town* (2001), which have included some of the John Mills photos. Few are duplicated in the selection for this new book, which surveys colonial Queensland, sorted by geographic regions and largely from the 1870s when the colony was still expanding north and westwards. The images allow us a window into Queensland's past and are accompanied by short descriptions to provide context. They show Brisbane as a rudimentary town with a few grand buildings such as Parliament House, and a bush community scattered around the colony, living in quite rough conditions. Who today would swap lives with Dr Handt on the Mount Britton goldfield in the early 1880s, or Hyland, an early settler at Stanthorpe in the 1870s, in his even smaller humpy. Another picture shows sugar planter John Spiller, a Mackay pioneer, living in a substantial but grass-thatched roofed house. Rural towns were full of wooden structures lining dirt roads, with hotels the only buildings of substance.

These are images of a Queensland now largely forgotten, except by individuals who possess collections of old family photos, and by historians. They deserve to be seen by more people and to be preserved on the public record. Lyall Ford has given us access to a world that has passed, for which we owe him thanks.

Clive Moore, Associate Professor
School of History, Philosophy, Religion and Classics
University of Queensland

John Henry and Mary Ann Loisa Mills, 1880s

Acknowledgements

Dianne Byrne in her book A Travelling Photographer in Colonial Queensland has documented the activities of William Boag, who with his partner, John Henry Mills, travelled widely around Queensland in the early 1870s taking and developing photographs for sale to the public. I would like to acknowledge her research as it has assisted me in the compilation of the Introduction for this book.

Late in 1875, Mills formed a new partnership with Albert Reckitt and they continued to travel around Queensland as professional photographers. Some of the albums they produced are in public libraries, in particular the National Library of Australia (NLA) in Canberra, the John Oxley Library (JOL) in Brisbane and the Mackay City Council Library in Mackay. Other photographs are in the possession of Mills descendants, in particular Keith Mills and myself. The photographs in this book are a representative sample of photographs from these collections. Where a library has been sourced, this has been acknowledged below the particular photograph.

For assistance with the historical research, I acknowledge the staff of the Queensland State Library in Brisbane and the libraries of Balonne Shire Council in St George, Bauhinia Shire Council in Springsure, Warroo Shire Council in Surat and Hinchinbrook Shire Council in Ingham. Others who have provided assistance include Peter Keegan from Roma, Jean Turvey, Ken Treloar and Keith and Val Mills from Mackay. Where information has been obtained from copyrighted publications, this is acknowledged below the particular photograph.

In 2001, a Sydney businessman, Kevin Maloney, realised the historical significance of the Mills photographs and, using originals provided by Keith Mills and myself, established the Pioneer Tracks of Queensland Gallery at the Marley Accommodation Centre in Nebo, west of Mackay. It houses a collection of over one hundred framed and mounted Mills photographs and is well worth a visit by anyone interested in Queensland's history and heritage. His practical and financial support and encouragement in the production of this book is gratefully acknowledged.

I would also like to thank Dr Clive Moore for contributing the Foreword and acknowledge Annette Baxter for her desktop publishing skills and Robert Bottger for producing the map.

Lyall Ford

Introduction

When John Henry Mills died peacefully in 1919 at 68 years of age, a short obituary in Mackay's Daily Mercury referred to his life as a gold miner at Mount Britton, a deserted gold mining township northwest of Mackay. There was no mention of his earlier life as a travelling photographer when, in partnership with firstly William Boag and then Albert Reckitt, he created an invaluable visual record of life in the newly formed colony of Queensland. Only now is the importance of his contribution to the recording of Queensland's history being recognised.

John emigrated from England to Brisbane with his parents in 1865 at 14 years of age. His father, Joseph, had been a silk weaver in Coventry but when this industry collapsed during the 1860s, he was forced out of the industry. Menial work as a gardener did not satisfy him and concern about the miserable weather and poor living conditions, which had resulted in the death of their first two infants, led he and his wife Sarah to join the thousands of emigrants making their way to Australia. Tragedy struck the family during a miserable voyage out on the 'Lobelia'. Sarah became ill and, after suffering for eight weeks, died while the ship was anchored in Moreton Bay awaiting clearance to land in Brisbane. Sailors from the ship buried her in a lonely grave on Mud Island. As there had been a number of deaths on board due to typhoid, Joseph and the children then had to tolerate a further month in quarantine, in prison-like conditions at Dunwich on North Stradbroke Island.

John Henry Mills in a Police uniform at a reunion attended in the late 1870s
Reckitt & Mills

The family settled in Brisbane and in the late 1860s, John Mills became a police officer. The main task of the police force at that time was to control the Aboriginal population and at 4pm each day police would ride along Queen Street cracking stockwhips to signal to the Aboriginals that it was time to leave the town and move back to their encampments on the fringes of the settlement. One of John Mills' duties was the enforcement of law and order at one of their camps at Enoggera.

In about 1871, he accepted a transfer to Pimpama, between Brisbane and the Gold Coast, where he became a bailiff at the Beenleigh Court of Petty Sessions. In 1872, he met up with a travelling photographer, William Boag, who had moved from New South Wales to southeast Queensland in October of the previous year. He had worked his way round the southern shores of Moreton Bay, taking in the Logan, Albert and Pimpama Rivers and in February was based at Yatala. Dianne Byrne, in her book about the life and work of Boag, explains how he operated:

> The portable darkroom was essential to Boag's operation. It was horse drawn and was designed to accommodate all the equipment required for the collodian or wet plate process, which produced a negative on a plate of glass. This process required the operator to pour emulsion onto a glass plate by hand, expose it while wet and then develop it immediately, making it essential that he have ready access to his equipment and his stock of chemicals. Using this vehicle, Boag was able to work for days in the most remote locations, producing wet plate negatives (measuring approx. 8 x 11 cms) which (unlike earlier daguerreotypes) had the great advantage of being able to generate unlimited numbers of finely-detailed paper prints. These prints could be tinted, coloured or otherwise

finished according to the requirements of the customer, and they could be produced in a variety of sizes, the most popular appearing to be cartes-de-visites (paper prints mounted on card, measuring around 6 x 9 cms). The carte was especially attractive because it was durable, portable and relatively cheap, making it the perfect medium for bringing photography to a wider, working class audience.

The Albert River near Beenleigh, c1872

Boag & Mills

Mills became so interested in Boag's photographic work that he resigned from the Police force and took on the role of agent for Boag, planning his visits and coordinating appointments. 'John H. Mills' was listed as a manager of the company and his name began to feature in newspaper advertisements. During the autumn of 1872, Boag stayed at the Ferry Hotel at Yatala. He made short trips to Brisbane and to Nerang Creek taking photographs, returning to the hotel in mid-May.

He and Mills then toured the Albert and Logan areas. By then, Mills was taking and developing photographs himself. In his personal collection, there are two photographs of the Albert River near the Beenleigh sugar plantation, which were probably taken on this trip. He has placed them side-by-side to produce a wide-angle lens appearance. Note that the same boat appears in both halves of the photo. Yellowwood Mountain can be seen in the distance on the left hand side.

In mid-year, Boag and Mills left for Brisbane, stopping briefly on the way to take more photographs at Cleveland. They now called themselves 'Boag & Mills' and the 'Australian Photographic Company'. In the city, they photographed a number of the principal businesses, public buildings and private dwellings. From there they moved to the new tin mining township of Stanthorpe near the New South Wales border, where they remained until the end of March 1873, covering every aspect of the settlement and the mining operations. Extracts from an article in the Border Post and Stannum Miner at that time read as follows:

Boag & Mills insignia

> We took our "last fond look" at the album of the Australian Photographic Company on Wednesday last, as Messrs Boag and Mills, the representatives of that company in this part of Queensland, intend leaving Stanthorpe on Monday next for Warwick, en route to join their partners in the north ... The views of claims and buildings in this district, taken by the artists alluded to are really first-class, the smallest object standing out in bold relief. Being acquainted with many of the claims photographed, we could easily distinguish the workings, and even the faces of many of those employed.

They remained in Warwick for a few weeks before moving north and late in June 1873 arrived in the North Queensland town of Mackay, which became their base for the next three years. They spent the first few days taking photographs of well-known places in the town and showed these to the proprietors of the Mackay Mercury. The editor's comments in the paper included:

> The work produced by these artists surpasses in cleaness and finish all that has been hitherto executed in Mackay, and we can recommend those who desire to secure really first-class photographs to pay a visit to Messrs. Boag & Mills.

Ten weeks after their arrival the editor was still enthusiastic:

> The specimens shewn to us of these artists' skill in photography are really excellent, more especially those which represent picturesque localities, rural homesteads with their surroundings, tin mining, public establishments, &c.

Their photographic work was certainly professional, both in the way that the photographs were set up and in their longevity. Many of the photos taken by Boag & Mills 130 years ago are almost as clear today as they would have been then, contrary to the state of many other photographs from that era and much later periods. They included people in their photographs wherever possible, especially in landscape views, to provide a sense of scale and to add an element of human interest to the vista captured by their lens. They took pains to ensure the right pose or placement of their subjects and frequently set up tableau groups, juxtaposing young and old, and active and passive figures, to obtain a diversity of appearance.

During their time in Mackay, the nearby sugar plantations provided a ready source of subject matter. Photos of Foulden, Pleystowe and River Estate plantations and the South Sea Islanders that worked on them have been preserved in libraries and private collections. Groups of Aboriginals and portraits of townsfolk were also popular topics. Many of the glass plate negatives from the early days at Cleveland up to this time in the Mackay district have been preserved and over 100 of them have been reproduced in Dianne Byrne's book. As each negative has been numbered in sequence, it is relatively easy to follow the course of their travels around Queensland.

Albert Reckitt insignia, 1875

Late in 1873, gold was discovered at the Palmer River in Far North Queensland and a rush quickly followed. Cooktown became a thriving seaport and in May 1874, Mills travelled there by steamer and set up a studio, advertising his presence in the *Cooktown Herald*. After a successful few weeks, he packed his belongings and returned to Mackay where he again met up with Boag. They resumed their activities until October 1875 when Mills again visited Cooktown. This time he met Albert Reckitt, another professional photographer who had established a studio there earlier that year. Although there was a big age difference, with Albert being 46 and

John only 24, a strong friendship quickly developed. Reckitt, who had given up cane farming at Maryborough to become a professional photographer, advertised regularly in the *Cooktown Herald* from 28 May to 15 December 1875.

It was about this time that Boag & Mills split up and went their separate ways. John Mills and Albert Reckitt then formed another partnership. They settled in Mackay where they re-established the previous Boag & Mills studio in North-street (now River Street) opposite the Catholic Church. There they produced hundreds of portraits of local and visiting residents during the next five years, using the names 'Reckitt & Mills' and 'The Queensland Photographic Company'.

Reckitt & Mills insignia, 1876–1897

They also set up a portable darkroom on the back of a buggy similar to the one that Boag & Mills had used and in 1877 they set off on a long trip through the colony. They produced portraits and landscape photographs, especially shots of individual establishments with the owners posing in front, and sold them to the public either as individual prints, groups of prints, cartes-de-visites or in specially produced albums. Many people sent the albums to their relatives and friends in the Motherland to give them an idea of what life was like in the colonies. Each year, for the next three years, they undertook other trips around the colony. In 1879, they were in Maryborough for a few weeks in March and April.

They carried their tent, supplies and photographic equipment in the buggy. Roads were almost non-existent, consisting only of bullock wagon tracks winding through the bush. They visited Brisbane, Roma, St George, Surat, Charleville, Tambo, Blackall, Aramac, Springsure and Clermont, and recorded scores of scenes on film. They called in at some of the large sheep and cattle stations, including Amby Downs near Mitchell, Mount Abundance near Roma and Bowen Downs, north of Aramac. One of the albums from their 1877 trip, showing scenes of the Roma - St George area, is in the John Oxley Library in Brisbane.

Before the introduction of the dry plate process in 1879, exposure times ranged from fifteen seconds to one minute, so it was important that the subjects remained motionless for that length of time. When sitting for portraits, adults' heads were held in head clamps rigged up on the chairs behind their heads where they could not be seen. Keeping children perfectly still for that length of time was an art in itself and the photographer would use various tricks to keep the child's attention, eg, blowing a toy trumpet. The same requirement applied to the people (and animals) posing in streetscapes and in front of buildings. 'Ghosts' would appear in the photo if movement occurred during the exposure.

It is apparent that the partners had a wry wit. In any photos involving themselves or their equipment, someone is wearing an old fashioned (even then) English pith helmet as a prop, or there is as old-fashioned flintlock rifle.

The photographic process required the use of many different chemicals, and some knowledge of chemistry was important. Albert kept a quarto size notebook into which he recorded details of the various chemical concoctions that he used in the business as well as for other general uses. The partners had special albums made up by Watson Ferguson & Co. with subtitles printed on each page. They would then paste in the appropriate landscape and streetscape photos.

In March 1879 the *Mackay Standard* reported as follows:

> Messrs. Reckitt and Mills having completed extensive alterations to their studio in North-street are now taking really first-class pictures, both portraits and views. They have also a fine collection of Queensland views taken during a long tour through the colony, and anyone desirous of filling up a photo scrap album could scarcely hope for a better opportunity. The work of this firm shows that they are not only in possession of the best instruments required for turning out good pictures, but that they are also able to use them for something better than the ordinary style of soot and white-wash productions which are too often accepted as triumphs of photographic art. Messrs. Reckitt and Mills inform us that they intend forming a separate album of Mackay and district views before leaving and if the pictures contained in it are as good as those to be seen at the gallery, it ought to prove a remunerative speculation.

Four copies of this album entitled 'Views of Mackay' are in the Mackay City Council Library.

Albert Reckitt, c1898
H.W. Salmon, Winchester

Edith Mary Reckitt, 1890s
H W Salmon, Winchester

Reckitt & Mills ran regular advertisements in the *Standard* from then until 23 May 1879. They also advertised in all issues of the *Mackay Mercury* between 19 March and 14 May 1879 stating, 'Portraits taken in the latest style and finish' and 'Views taken, either town or country'. They also advertised their 'Splendid collection of western views'. At the Annual Show conducted by the Mackay Agricultural, Pastoral and Mining Association in 1879, Reckitt & Mills entered photographs in the Landscape Photography section. They won a prize, which was a small but impressive bronze medal. On 23 May, their advertisement had an additional sentence - 'The Studio will positively be closed next week' - and there were no more advertisements that year.

They then headed off on another of their trips around the colony. Two townships that they visited intermittently were Clermont and Copperfield. In the Clermont district, gold had been found in widely distributed alluvial deposits and some small-scale reef mining was being carried on. Copper had been discovered at Copperfield in 1861 and the mining company operated until 1879 but the population decreased rapidly during the 1870s. They encountered hundreds of people on their various trips around the colony and met Thomas Butcher Ricketts and his family on their visits to Copperfield and Clermont. Although the second eldest daughter was only 15 years of age in 1880, it seems that she may have already attracted the eye of the older bachelor, John Henry Mills.

Scores of Reckitt & Mills photographs from their various trips have been preserved in libraries and private collections. Many books and other documents published over the years have reproduced Reckitt & Mills photographs, usually without acknowledgment of the photographers. It is a pity that the current owners of old photographs, who require their own ownership to be acknowledged, do not always advise the name of the photographers so that they can also be acknowledged.

Reckitt & Mills retained their base in Mackay until 1881 when gold was discovered at Mount Britton north of Nebo. They joined the early rush and set up a photographic studio as they had many times in the past, but this time things were to work out quite differently. They became caught up in the excitement of the rush and became miners themselves, subsequently coming to love the beautiful setting in which they found themselves and making it their long-term home. They still produced photographs, and succeeding generations are fortunate that they did so, as they have provided a detailed pictorial record of life on an early Queensland gold mining field.

The Mills family, 1896 – Ethel, Edie, Mary Ann Louisa, Bert, Cyril, John Henry

Reckitt & Mills

Another of the early visitors to the Mount Britton field was Thomas Butcher Ricketts, accompanied by one of his daughters, Mary Ann Louisa. She and Mills struck up a friendship and kept in contact after she returned to Clermont. A proposal followed during 1882 and in October, Mary made the long 300-kilometre journey from Clermont to Mount Britton by buggy over rough bullock wagon tracks. They were married at the field where they remained for the next 25 years, raising a family of six children. Their first child, Albert Mount Britton (Bert) Mills, was born on 30 September 1883. He was the first white child born in the vicinity and to mark the occasion his father planted a fig tree, which today is a prominent feature at the site. Their other children were Ethel (grandmother of the author), Edith Mary, Cyril Whetstone, Flora Alice and Maud Emma.

Early in the rush, Reckitt & Mills pegged a Prospecting Claim and named it the 'Edith Mary' after Albert Reckitt's daughter who had been taken back to England by Reckitt after his wife died in 1866. In the first few years, the mine flourished and produced some excellent returns. The partners entered some samples in the 1886 Colonial and Indian Exhibition at South Kensington in England and received an award of a medal and a magnificent certificate signed.

Shortage of water, inadequate returns and lack of capital to develop the mines gradually brought about the demise of the township and families slowly departed. Beekeeping became the main source of income for the Mills family. Diaries recorded by Mills reveal how incredibly harsh living conditions were at Mount Britton in those days. A photograph taken by Albert Reckitt in 1896 shows the family at their home, Cairnedie. Mary was pregnant with Flora, who was born on Christmas Eve that year.

During 1897, Albert Reckitt returned to England to live with Edith Mary his two sisters who had raised his daughter. He thought that he may not return to Mount Britton so the Reckitt & Mills partnership was dissolved at this time. After several months, he decided that he could not handle the English weather any longer and returned to spend his remaining years with the Mills family. The Mills children loved Albert and thought of him as a second father. They called him Leckie. In 1905, he died at 75 years of age and was buried at the Mount Britton cemetery. John Mills, his partner and friend for 30 years, provided a headstone, which is still in place.

Mills family, c1911
Standing: Edie, Flora, Bert, Ethel, Maud
Seated: Cyril, John Henry, Mary Ann Louisa

By 1908, only two families remained at the field – the Mills and Burgess families. Mills finally succumbed to the inevitable when the hard physical labour, the absence of an adequate income, the need to travel regularly to Mackay for medical attention and the impending marriage of the eldest daughter, Ethel, led him to give in to his wife's wishes and relocate to Mackay. There he obtained work as a storeman at Lamberts Pty Ltd. He also became the Sunday School Superintendent at Holy Trinity Church of England.

The 1918 cyclone in Mackay provided him with a final opportunity to use his photographic skills before he died in 1919 at 67 years of age.

John Henry Mills was typical of many of our pioneers, who, along with his wife, bore the heat and burden of the day without complaint. They loved their family and raised them to the best of their ability. They worshipped the Lord and brought their children up as Christians in difficult times. My book 'Below These Mountains' tells the full story of John Henry Mills and his family.

Mills loved Mount Britton and strove to develop the area so that it would provide a home for future Mills generations. This did not happen in his lifetime but who knows what the future may bring. In the meantime, he will long be remembered for his photographic work, which has provided hundreds of unique images of our pioneers and their way of life. Copies of his photographs will be preserved and serve to remind future generations of his skill and dedication.

Holy Trinity Church group, c1915 (John Henry Mills, Sunday School Superintendent, in centre; Flora behind him)

Site of Mount Britton township, 1958

Bob Smith

Plate 1

Parliament House from the Botanic Gardens, Brisbane, mid-1870s

The Colonial Architect, Charles Tiffin, designed this impressive French Renaissance style Parliament House building to take full advantage of its splendid site overlooking the Botanic Gardens and Queen's Park.

When the Colony of Queensland came into existence in 1859, the white population was about 28,000, including about 4,000 living in Brisbane. A campaign by Governor Bowen to attract immigrants resulted in 38,000 arrivals between January 1860 and September 1865. In parallel with these arrivals, a vast development program was begun using borrowed funds from London. This work reached a peak during 1865 when the first railway was opened between Ipswich and Grandchester, Cobb & Co. established an office in Brisbane and started its first run between Brisbane and Ipswich, the first Brisbane shops were lit by gas, and in July, the foundations were laid for this magnificent building to house Queensland's first elected Parliament.

Ford, BTM p24
Hogan & Winkle, QHS p17

Plate 2

View of Brisbane from Bowen Terrace, mid-1870s

Here is evidence of the rapid growth that occurred in Brisbane in the first fifteen years after the Colony of Queensland was formed. In the centre foreground is Petrie Bight, where the number of ships tied up at the Howard Smith and Government wharves illustrates the important role that shipping played in the development of the infant colony. The gas works is situated behind the wharves. To the left of the photo, the new Parliament House building is an imposing structure, dwarfing all other buildings in the city.

NLA Album 261/130

Plate 3

Victoria Bridge from the north bank of the Brisbane River, mid-1870s

In June 1874, ten years after the calling of tenders, the Marquis of Normanby, Governor of Queensland, opened this impressive steel bridge over the Brisbane River amidst great celebration. There had already been some development on the south bank of the river, but the completion of this bridge greatly boosted activity on that side. Note the complete absence of traffic when this photo was taken.

Construction had begun in 1864 and a temporary wooden bridge was completed in June 1865 to act as staging for the permanent structure. This happened a few days before John Mills arrived in Moreton Bay from Coventry, England. However, marine borers ravaged the piles of the temporary structure and half of it collapsed in November 1867. Financial troubles further delayed completion of the new bridge, as did a flood in 1873 that damaged the unfinished structure and wrecked the temporary bridge.

NLA Album 261/128

Plate 4

Brisbane Hospital at the site of the present Royal Brisbane Hospital in Bowen Bridge Road at Herston, mid-1870s

When this building opened in January 1867, at what was then known as 'The Quarries', the patients, bedding and equipment were transferred from the old Moreton Bay Hospital, situated near the present Supreme Court building in George Street, in a motley collection of cabs, wagons and drays. In that year, 654 inpatients and 4141 outpatients were treated, with 47 patients dying. The greatest scourges in those early years were typhoid fever and tuberculosis. During 1876, 123 patients died, of whom only nine were aged over 60 years.

Plate 5

Ornamental Pond, Bowen Park, Brisbane, opposite the present Royal Brisbane Hospital, mid-1870s

The lush detailed plantings and the use of water elements and sculpture are apparent in this photograph showing the entrance to the Acclimatisation Gardens.

This area of 16 hectares, formerly worked as a brickfield, was granted to the Queensland Acclimatisation Society between 1862 and 1865. This society was a socially and politically influential organisation concerned with the importation and trial of plant species, although some animals were also trialled into the unfamiliar sub-tropical climate of the new colony. The grounds also functioned as a 'place of public resort'. It was named Bowen Park in honour of the first governor of Queensland and initial patron of the Queensland Acclimatisation Society, Sir George Ferguson Bowen. The Brisbane City Council purchased the property in 1914 and subsequently sold a number of parcels to the Royal National Agricultural and Industrial Association. Today an area of 1.7 hectares remains as a park.

Plate 6

Webster & Co. Ltd, Mary Street, Brisbane, mid-1870s

Webster & Co. were merchants, importers and commission agents, and the Queensland agents for Crossleys kerosene oil engines. The firm was first listed in the Queensland Post Office Directories in 1874 so would probably have begun operations a year or two earlier.

These stationary oil engines were very simple with few working parts, and preceded the invention of the four cylinder internal combustion engine. They were specially designed for agricultural and general purposes and were suitable for driving equipment such as pumps, chaffcutters and circular saws.

Plate 7

View of Brisbane from Windmill Hill looking towards Mt Cootha, mid-1870s

The building on the left is the original Brisbane Boys Grammar School on the site of the present Roma Street Railway Station. It opened in 1869 but as early as 1874 the subscribers and trustees began to think about shifting because of encroachment by the railway line from Ipswich as it neared completion. The school moved to its present site on Gregory Terrace in 1881.

Windmill Hill took its name from the old convict-built windmill, later known as the Observatory, located on Wickham Terrace. It was an ideal location from which to view the city, which grew rapidly after the new colony of Queensland was formed in 1859. During 1860, for example, 160 new houses were built in nine months, the majority of them on Windmill Hill.

Logan & Watson, SS p156

Plate 8

All Saints' Church of England, Wickham Terrace, Brisbane, mid-1870s

The Governor of Queensland, Sir Samuel Wensley Blackall, laid the foundation stone for this church in April 1869 and the Bishop of Brisbane named it 'All Saints'. The opening services were held in September of that year. The style is early English Gothic Revival. At that time, the Mills family lived at Kelvin Grove and would have attended this church. John Mills took this photo when he returned to Brisbane on one of his trips as a professional photographer a few years later.

This building replaced an earlier church built by Bishop Tufnel in 1862 to serve the growing population on Windmill Hill and Spring Hill. It became known as the Wickham Terrace District Church and Rev. John Tomlinson was the first incumbent. Within a few years of its construction, it became apparent that it needed to be demolished, so it was pulled down and this new one built in its place.

PLATE 9

Interior of All Saints' Church, Wickham Terrace, mid-1870s

The interior of this church is delightful and the hammer beam roof truss system is one of the few in Australia. The walls were constructed of porphyry stone from Petrie's local quarry and are 500 mm thick. Looking towards the altar and the beautiful stained glass windows of this impressive church, a large pipe organ is visible on the right. As with most churches the pews, transferred from the previous building, were made for durability not comfort.

During the building of the church in 1869, several gifts for the interior were received. For the chancel, the architect donated a stone sedilia (a seat for the officiating clergy in the recess in the south wall); Dr Hugh Bell and the children of the late Mr T.S. Warry gave the stone pulpit in Mr Warry's memory; and Mr Tout provided a carpet for the chancel. Funds were insufficient however to provide a new font or new pews.

Hogan, BQH p13

Plate 10

Freemason's Ball in the first School of Arts building on the corner of Queen and Creek Streets, Brisbane, 1872

Three photographs have been joined together to provide this composite view. John Mills took these immediately after a Masonic Ball. A description of a similar Grand Masonic Ball held at the School of Arts in Ipswich in 1866 explained, 'On the platform were arranged all the furniture of a regularly constituted Lodge. The Chairs of the Master and Wardens, with various emblems of Royal Arch Masonry, occupied this part of the hall.' This explains the arrangement of furniture on the stage for this 1872 Brisbane ball, as it would have been similar.

The ball was probably promoted by the District Grand Lodge (English Constitution) or one of the Provincial Grand Lodges (Irish and Scottish Constitutions) on behalf of all the Brisbane lodges. The Freemasons would have hired the School of Arts for the occasion.

Plate 11

Pullen's cottage at Enoggera on the outskirts of Brisbane, mid-1870s

Mr and Mrs Pullen are working in the garden of their cottage with its timber shingled roof and paling fence. They maintained a vineyard here. Many people tried to emulate the gardens they had left behind in the old country, and took great pride in keeping them neat and tidy. The cottage is typical of the better standard of cottages in the area at the time.

Shingles were a popular roofing material in Queensland in the 1800s. They were cut from a variety of bush timbers, including various species of eucalypt, casuarina and stringybark and lasted for at least ten years.

Evans, AH p36

Plate 12

Grandchester railway station, the oldest railway station building in Queensland, mid-1870s

A horse rider faces the camera at the end of the loading ramp in the middle foreground while a second looks on. To the right an empty wagon waits in a siding. In July 1865, this railway line was the first opened in Queensland during a period of rapid development in the new colony. It ran from Ipswich, the highest navigable point on the Brisbane River's tributary, the Bremer, to this station, known then as Bigge's Camp. At the opening ceremony, Governor Bowen suggested a name change to Grandchester, from the Latin words 'grand' meaning big, and 'castra' meaning a camp. This idea was adopted soon afterwards.

The former name originated in 1842 after Frederick and Francis Bigge camped at the local lagoon on their way to establish Mount Brisbane Station. Soon afterwards, the teamsters taking supplies inland and bringing back wool and other goods to Brisbane for export began to camp there regularly. After the railway opened, settlers were able to send their products by rail from Grandchester to Ipswich, thence by barge down the Brisbane River to the Port of Brisbane.

Plate 13

Laidley railway station, west of Grandchester, mid-1870s

This building is a similar type of construction to many of the houses at the time. The timber frame and galvanised iron cladding were prefabricated in Great Britain and shipped to Queensland for assembly on site. Many thought that it was too extravagant for its relatively isolated location. When it was completed in 1866 one Government member said that it 'looked more like a gentleman's villa in England than a railway station, and was scarcely used except for the supply of firewood to the engine'. A visitor in 1876 said that it was quite large enough for a town like Ipswich but 'there it stands, a monument to the folly of our immediate ancestors'.

James Laidley arrived in Australia from England in 1814. One of his sons subsequently moved to Queensland and the township of Laidley was named after him.

Plate 14

Gatton railway station, mid-1870s

The signal is set on 'Stop' while the passengers await the arrival of the passenger train that will take them on their journey. The timber shingles on the roof show that it was built in Queensland, unlike the much grander Laidley station.

This railway line extending westwards from Grandchester, through Laidley to Gatton, opened in June 1866. It included two tunnels through the Liverpool Range. The newly opened line was a popular means of transport as it was much more comfortable than riding in horse-drawn buggies or sulkies on the rough roads of the infant colony.

Plate 15

Gatton railway bridge, mid-1870s

This steel girder bridge, constructed in the first half of 1866, spans Lockyer Creek on the western side of the town. The materials were imported from Great Britain, unlike smaller bridges at the time, which were constructed with local timber.

Still in use today, it is on the Gatton to Helidon section of line, which opened on 30 July 1866. The remaining section to Toowoomba opened on 1 May 1867. It was not until 1875 that a line was established between Brisbane and Ipswich, thus completing the link from Toowoomba to Brisbane.

Plate 16

Groom's Pioneer Bakery in Griggs Street, Stanthorpe, 1872

This small weatherboard building with timber shingles on the roof housed two businesses. Groom's fresh bread loaves are visible in his window and a range of watches can be seen in W. Groth's window, shaded by a calico awning.

The discovery of large deposits of tin near Stanthorpe in March 1872 prompted a panic among mining speculators and a huge rush to the field ensued. The nearest supplies had to come from Warwick, 60 kilometres to the north, so business-minded people took advantage of the situation and made their money providing goods and services to the hungry miners. Boag and Mills arrived on the field early in November 1872, subsequently photographing all the buildings in the township and many of the mining activities.

Byrne, TPCQ p 80

Plate 17

Sluicing alluvial tin, Stanthorpe, 1872-73

This creek has been dammed to capture the trickle of water and a 'gated sluice' constructed on the dam wall. Wheelbarrows are used to transport the alluvium to the head of the sluice for washing in order to separate the tin.

Although too much water was a nuisance, a reliable water supply was essential in all alluvial mining operations to facilitate the separation of the heavy metal from the alluvium, so a stream was often dammed or diverted to obtain enough water.

Plate 18

Hyland's humpy near Stanthorpe, 1872-73

Reuben and Abraham Mills (brothers of John) and William Bynon (their brother-in-law) travelled to Stanthorpe while Boag & Mills were working there. Here they are visiting Hyland at his rudimentary humpy. Reuben and Abraham later settled in the Boonah district southwest of Brisbane. The Bynon family settled at Samford on the north-western outskirts of Brisbane, later moving to Fordham near Grantham.

Humpies like this, made from a variety of easily obtained materials, were common in the early months of new mining discoveries.

Ford, BTM p52

Plate 19

Unloading a cart bogged to the axles a few kilometres east of Stanthorpe on the road to Sugarloaf, near the Queensland/New South Wales border, 1872-73

This is a typical Queensland wet weather scene in pioneering times where two travellers have to unload the heavy cargo from a cart to ease the burden on their horse after the cart became bogged to the axles in a creek crossing.

Many roads were nothing more than two rutted wagon wheel tracks winding through the countryside, with trips being measured in days, weeks or, sometimes, months. Bridges, floodways and culverts were practically non-existent. River and creek crossings presented a major challenge during the wet season and roads were often closed for months.

Plate 20

Sydney Street, Mackay, looking north towards the Pioneer River, 1876

Buildings on the right include Mrs Cook's Royal Hotel, the *Mackay Standard* office, the saddler McKenney, Wills Hotel on the corner of Victoria Street, and George Ricketts' Hotel on another corner in the right foreground. The road has been formed up in the middle to drain water into grassed drains along the sides, but the unpaved roads of most Queensland towns were dusty when dry and muddy when wet.

The township of Port Mackay had been established for only eleven years when Boag & Mills arrived towards the end of June 1873, by which time the population had increased to about 1000 people. There was no bridge over the river when this photo was taken. The Sydney Street bridge was constructed at the end of this street the following year.

Plate 21

Aboriginals in a cane field, Mackay district, ca 1873

This Boag & Mills photograph of a group of Aboriginals was one of those used by H. Ling Roth in his book *The Discovery and Settlement of Port Mackay, Queensland*, published in England in 1908.

It seems that Mackay's Aboriginals were highly regarded by the European population. An 1882 report in the *Mackay Mercury*, referring to the annual distribution of blankets said, 'The men were tall, healthy and stalwart looking, the women cleanly, and civilised in appearance. Any with whom we conversed were able to speak in remarkably good English, some of them in fact speaking as if that language were their native tongue.'

Ford, BTM p54

Plate 22

Indentured South Sea Islanders at Pleystowe sugar plantation, Mackay, mid-1870s

There were many large sugar plantations in the Mackay district, each with its own mill. Pacific Islanders, known then as Kanakas, were brought from their homelands by recruiting vessels to supply labour. There are over 80 of them in this photo.

The growing and milling of sugarcane was the biggest industry in the district and by 1877, Mackay had become the largest sugar-producing centre in Queensland. Despite allegations of abuse and mistreatment, thousands of islanders were brought into Queensland and their labour became vital to the sugar industry.

Byrne, TPCQ p 110

Plate 23

Back Row: Frank Smith (Solicitor), ..., Henry Brandon (Manager AJS Bank), ..., Percy Crees (nephew of J. Spiller), Geo. Smith (Shipping Agent)
Front Row: Mrs H Brandon, Mrs F. Smith, John Spiller, Mrs Spiller, Mrs G. Smith

The original house at Pioneer plantation owned by John Spiller and John Crees, Mackay, ca 1875

This photograph shows a group of well-known Mackay identities relaxing in front of the house. Spiller is generally recognised as the first person to have successfully grown sugar cane in the Mackay district, having planted cuttings brought from Java in June 1865. The house would have been built some time after that. The roofs of these early houses were thatched, which was somewhat of a fire hazard. Spiller dismantled the building in 1878 and replaced it with a grand residence measuring 24 metres by 25 metres on high stumps.

Bank managers often became personally involved in the businesses that their banks were financing and the manager of the A.J.S. bank in Mackay, Henry Brandon, was intimately involved in Spiller's affairs and became his financial partner. The solicitor, Frank Smith, was also actively involved in many businesses.

Roth, PMQ p61
Kerr, PP pp27, 43
Bolton, TMA p73

Plate 34

To-Kalon House, the home of a sugar planter, Ingham, ca 1875

This house is different to the normal Queenslander style with its massive thatched roof copied from the colonial bungalows of the Raj in India. Many of the planters had Indian connections.

Located on the southern outskirts of what is now Ingham, its design assists air circulation to provide cooling in the hot, humid North Queensland climate.

NLA Album 260/5

Plate 35

View of Charters Towers from the General Wyndham works, ca 1875

Workers at the General Wyndham in the foreground have a commanding view over the settlement, which at this early stage in the development of Charters Towers seems to consist of shanties scattered at random across the countryside. By 1877, however, businessmen began to realise that this was now a permanent settlement and substantial buildings started to appear.

Three young prospectors, Hugh Mosman, James Fraser and George Clarke, discovered gold at Charters Towers early in 1872. A rush followed and by the end of that year, 3,000 miners had flocked to the area. The 91,265 ounces of gold sent out by escort during 1872 accounted for more than half the total Queensland output. Two centres developed – Millchester, about five kilometres to the west, and the Towers (known then as 'Upper Camp'). For a while, it appeared that Millchester would become the larger of the two but leads petered out and the emphasis returned to Charters Towers, named after the Gold Commissioner, W.S. Charters. By 1876, the population of the twin centres was approaching 7,000 and the number of hotels had grown to 60.

Bolton, TMA p50
Springer, CTC pp 9–11

NLA Album 260/18

Plate 36

The Mystery claim, Charters Towers, ca 1875

A crowd of workers and onlookers has gathered at the head of the shaft for this photograph. The shed in the foreground houses the winding gear.

The year 1876 was the first for which authorities kept authentic records of gold production. These show that 35,355 tons of stone produced 52,585 ounces of gold. The Mystery Prospecting Claim, shown here, was one of the claims that produced good yields. In the month of June 1877 it produced 353 ounces of gold from 150 tons of stone.

NLA Album 260/23

Plate 37

Craven's crushing machine, Charters Towers, ca 1875

Richard Craven was a well-known miner at Charters Towers. In the 1870s, he owned this small crushing plant, one of twelve crushing mills on the field. Horses brought the ore to the mill for crushing in carts that tipped backwards, like the one on the left.

In 1886, Craven took up a claim in country that was generally considered to be unlikely ground. Spurning the wisdom of more experienced hands, he succeeded in gaining support for his plan to sink deeper shafts and was soon able to form a company. Work continued intermittently for three years until 'Craven's Shaft' had become a local joke. However, in 1889 the whole of Charters Towers celebrated when the shaft bottomed on a fabulous reef. Cables flew around the world and a new company was formed, with Craven doing very well financially. Another company, formed in 1891 to develop Craven's Caledonia claim, subsequently produced nearly 40,000 ounces of gold.

NLA Album 260/21

Plate 38

Reckitt & Mills campsite at Cashmere station on the Maranoa River, St George, 1877

This is a typical camp that Reckitt & Mills set up each night while travelling around Queensland on their photographic expeditions. The buggy complete with darkroom stands by the tents, while Albert Reckitt pours himself a cuppa from the billy.

Cashmere Station is located on the St George-Mitchell Road, 23 kilometres north of St George in Queensland's southwest. It was one of the earliest properties taken up in the region and a native police station was situated there in the 1860s. In 1870, W.F. Kennedy, the lessee of the station, transferred the lease to the Peel River Land Company (London). Three years later, the proprietor was Robert McMicking, who may have still been there when the photographers passed through in 1877.

Ford, BTM pp49,60

Plate 39

John Mills relaxes in his tent with a pipe after a hard day's travel, 1877

Reckitt & Mills have chosen two appropriately placed trees to support the rope holding up their tent. A tarpaulin over the tent keeps it waterproof. Mills has his prop pith helmet beside him on the ground and his foot rests on a new Snider rifle. In the back of the tent, another pith helmet is perched atop a flintlock rifle, both of which are used as props in many of their photos.

Ford, BTM p62

Plate 40

St George's Bridge from the north, Balonne River, 1877

Three men relax in the riverbed at St George's Bridge, which is a natural rocky crossing in the Balonne. Major Thomas Mitchell made a base here during his 1846 expedition, during which he discovered the Warrego, Maranoa and Belyando Rivers. He arrived at this location on St George's Day, 23 April 1846, hence the name.

While he was camped at this spot, he invented the canvas waterbag. He was having trouble with his wooden receptacles for carrying water and, as an experiment, he sewed pieces of canvas together to make a bag, which he greased with mutton tallow. The experiment proved a success and this led to the introduction of canvas waterbags throughout Australia.

Pike, QF p51 *JOL APE 14/7*

Plate 41

Arthur Macalister's Commercial Hotel on The Terrace, St George, 1877

Macalister acquired this hotel in 1871 and retained it for ten years. Two years before that he built the town's first courthouse. He raised a family of daughters, who were taught privately and were joined by other children who paid a small fee. As a result, he later became recognised as the founder of the first school in St George.

St George's Bridge was an ideal camping spot for the early teamsters. By the beginning of the 1860s, the town of St George had begun to take shape on the eastern bank of the river, upstream of the crossing. When Reckitt & Mills took this photograph, the population had increased to about 400 people. In 1953, the Jack Taylor Weir, combined with a high level bridge, was constructed immediately upstream of the natural crossing. The population of the town has grown steadily and today it stands at about 1500. It is the largest inland town in Queensland never to have had a railway.

Nolan, RC pp47,51

Plate 42

Gulnarbar station, St George, 1877

The bark roof and timber chimney stand out on this station homestead. Consider also the amount of work required to set out the English-style garden with its timber edges and gravel pathways. The paucity of plants is presumably an indication of dry times. The man posing at the doorway is probably George Kirk, who was the proprietor at the time. Reckitt & Mills camped on this property during their visit to the area.

Gulnarbar is situated by a large lagoon called Bogardy, 15 kilometres south of St George on the Whyenbah Road. G.A. and J. Loder established it and used it as a fattening station until 1859 when they put it up for auction. A "For Sale" advertisement in 1862 shows that it had a frontage of 20 miles to the west bank of the Balonne River and included 4,000 head of cattle. The estimated grazing capability was 25,000 to 30,000 sheep or 6,000 cattle. When F.T. Gregory surveyed the township of St George in 1863, Messrs Cochrane and Moore owned Gulnarbar but George Kirk became the proprietor in 1872.

Armstrong, IMF p30

Plate 43

Burrowes Street, Surat, 1877

On the left of this photo there is a Draper, the sign in the middle reads, 'Post Office & Stable, Schott & Phillips', and to the right of that building is a hotel owned by M. Marshall.

The township of Surat is located beside the Balonne River, 120 kilometres north of St George. It had received its name by 1850, and the following year a weekly mail run began. The first Post Office opened in January 1852. Cobb & Co established a changing station in 1880 when the company won the contract for the mail service from Yuleba through Surat to St George. Their coaches became Surat's lifeline for the next 44 years. Changing stations were established about every 25 kilometres along coach routes to provide a meal break for the driver and passengers as well as a change of horses. The building in Surat still exists as a museum and a permanent reminder of the old coaching days. Today the population is about 500 people.

Taylor, CRD p10

Plate 44

The gatekeeper, his wife and their domestic servant in front of the gatekeeper's cottage at Mt Abundance station, 1877

Allan MacPherson established Mt Abundance station in 1847 beside a waterhole in Muckadilla Creek about three kilometres south of the peak of that name discovered by Mitchell. MacPherson and his team of hired men, teamsters, stockriders and shepherds drove 10,000 sheep and 1,000 head of cattle past St George's Bridge and pressed on for a further 150 miles to the northwest into a land of rolling downs and unusually-shaped bottle trees, which Mitchell had named Fitzroy Downs. The local Aboriginal tribe watched the building of the homestead and out-stations with considerable displeasure.

In April 1848, Ludwig Leichhardt passed through Mt Abundance on his ill-fated expedition towards the west, writing his last letter to the world at the little slab and bark out-station a short distance south from the present township of Muckadilla. After leaving Mt Abundance, his party was never seen again and his fate remains unknown. In September of that year, the Aboriginal tribes rose en masse and descended upon the lonely collection of huts, spearing four men and killing or driving off 4,000 sheep. With MacPherson absent at his home station on the Gwydir, 350 miles away, the other employees panicked and fled.

Pike, QF p51
Taylor, CRD pp8-9

Plate 45

Wagon teams loading out of the woolshed at Mt Abundance, 1877

The Scottish Australian Investment Company purchased Mt Abundance from Steven Spencer in 1869 and developed it into a profitable sheep station. The wagons shown here would have been on the road for up to three months on their trip to Brisbane and her export wharves. They superseded the earlier two-wheeled drays.

After the Aboriginal attack on Mt Abundance in 1848 the tribes in the region arose as if in alliance and many pioneers in isolated homesteads lost their lives. After 400 Tingum warriors launched a surprise attack and killed his two Aboriginal retainers, Allan MacPherson decided that he should send his sheep back to the Gwydir and keep Mt Abundance going as a cattle station, but the drovers bringing in fresh cattle were ambushed and two of them speared. Then two teamsters who were taking away two dray loads of wool in May 1849 were ambushed and killed, so he decided to quit the property. By then, he estimated that he had lost at least 10,000 head of stock. In 1857, he sold out to Stephen Spencer, who arrived the following year with cattle but no sheep. Spencer shifted the homestead to a site on Bungeworgorai Creek about eight kilometres WSW from the present site of Roma, but struggled to survive for twelve difficult years before he in turn sold out.

Pike, QF p52

Plate 46

The courthouse at Roma, 1877

This is one of the many substantial public buildings erected in Roma in the late 1860s and early 1870s. In April 1877, Reckitt & Mills set up a studio in the rear of Mr E. Bellgrove's Auction Room opposite the Post Office and stayed for several weeks. They advertised in the local newspaper, the Western Star, saying that arrangements could be made for taking views in town or country. During this time, they produced many photographs of the town and portraits of the residents.

The township dates back to 1862, when Thomas Reid erected the Fitzroy Hotel, a bark shanty, near the present Roma trucking yards. It was here that the north-south road to New South Wales crossed the main east-west road to the western country and good water was available near the original creek crossing. Other hotels followed and Surveyor McDowall pegged the township at the head of Bungil Creek in September. The new township was given the name of 'Roma' in honour of the wife of the first Governor of Queensland (Sir George Ferguson Bowen) who, before her marriage was the Countess Diamantina Roma.

Taylor, CRD pp19-20

Plate 47

McDowall Street, Roma, demonstrating one of the difficulties that faced pioneer photographers, 1877

This photograph, looking west along Roma's main street from its intersection with Charles Street, is of particular interest technically. It illustrates the difficulties that photographers had in the glass plate era before 1879, when the exposure time for the lens was between fifteen seconds and one minute (depending on the amount of light). Any movement produced ghost images. In this shot, two of the men in the middle of the street have not moved but a third one has paused in one location for a moment, then moved on a few paces and halted again. This action has caused the dog to turn its head to the right away from the camera and look at the men.

Looking at the buildings, businesses on the left include Bassett & Skinner, who were General Storekeepers and Wine & Spirit Merchants, a stationer, a bakery owned by Mr Faulkner, the Roma Auction Mart, a business owned by Mr C. Bradley, the Queen's Arms Hotel on the corner of Arthur Street, and the General Printing Office. In the distance on the corner of Hawthorn Street is the Sydney Hotel managed by Mr E. Cook. On the right are McPhellamy & McLauchlan, who were butchers and advertised 'Prime Salt Beef Always On Hand', then L.C. Johnson (saddler), J.W. Johnston & Co. (general storekeepers), and Arnold & McGoldrich (saddler).

Plate 48

Bottle tree on the Roma Town Reserve, 1877

This photograph shows a large bottle tree thought to have been on the northern side of the highway a few kilometres east of the township. It is not there today.

The Roma district is noted for its bottle trees, the botanical name being Brachychiton. They are quite distinct from the West Australian tree, the Baobab. The bottle tree does not have a hollow, natural reservoir of water but the inner wood is soft and fibrous and contains considerable amounts of water. Today over 100 of these trees line the town's Anzac Avenue, each tree representing a local soldier fallen in the Great War of 1914-18. This avenue follows three streets, Station, Wyndham and Bungil Streets, forming a trail from the railway station to the cenotaph next to the Cultural Centre.

Plate 49

Jimbour House near Dalby, 1877

Work began on this magnificent building in 1874 under the supervision of Mr Harry Ensor. The cedar came from the Bunya Mountains and other timbers included spotted gum, blue gum, ironbark, bunya, cypress, hoop pine and some satinwood. Only the Welsh slates for the roof were imported. The total cost was about £30,000, an enormous sum in those days. The house incorporated all the latest mod-cons, with both water and gas being laid on. Gas was generated from coal won from a mine on the property. Water was pumped to the top of a tower 40 feet high by the first windmill erected in Queensland. The building has been preserved and can be inspected.

Jimbour was a huge property when Thomas Bell purchased it in 1843 from Henry Scougall for the sum of £3200. In a good season, grasses and herbage five to six feet tall covered the great rolling plains. Bell, who had come to Australia in 1829 in charge of convicts, brought his family of three sons and two daughters to the property. A year later, he excised two other properties from it, reducing its size to about 211,000 acres. At that time, it carried 12,000 sheep. After their wooden slab house burned down in 1867, the Bells built a new two-storey residence of bluestone and cedar. It was finished in 1870 and the family occupied it until the present Jimbour House shown in this photograph was completed. When Thomas Bell died in 1874, his youngest son, Joshua Peter Bell, became the owner.

Plate 50

The township of Charleville with some of the local Aboriginals looking on, 1877

At this time, Charleville was quite small as the first building had been erected only twelve years earlier. The township grew quickly in the 1880s, however, when it became the location for the main Cobb & Co. coach-building factory in Australia, employing 40 coachbuilders. The dry conditions made it particularly suitable for coach building.

Edmund Kennedy was the first European explorer to pass through this area in 1847 while examining the newly discovered Victoria River, which he later named the Barcoo River after learning the name from the local Kunja Aboriginals. Others to follow included A.C. Gregory in 1858, searching for the trail of Ludwig Leichhardt, and William Landsborough in 1862, searching for the ill-fated Burke and Wills. Many selectors then took up runs in the district, one of these being Gowrie Station, which had its homestead at the corner of the present Watson and Burke Streets. As Charleville was located on a stock route leading from Western Queensland to New South Wales, it became a regular stopover for travellers and drovers. The first residents, Louis and Mary Janetzky, arrived in 1865. He was a builder and erected a hotel for Robert Cooper. Janetzky then opened a store and later on purchased the hotel himself.

Plate 51

A busy scene in Arthur Street, Tambo, 1877

When Reckitt & Mills took this photo, Tambo was the busiest town in the west, the commercial emporium of the interior. Traffic was so great in the main thoroughfare that a narrow strip down the centre was gravelled so that the wagons were able to traverse it in wet weather without being in danger of bogging in the black soil. On the left hand side of the road, buildings that can be identified include a business owned by G. Bredhauer, the Commercial Stores owned by H.T. Walsh, and a General Store owned by M.H. Bilton & Sons. On the right above the leading bullocks, there are signs identifying the Telegraph Hotel and the Queensland National Bank. Note that gas streetlights were being installed at the time.

Tambo lies on the banks of the Barcoo River about 210 kilometres north of Charleville. The builder of the first hotel in 1863 was William Coverley, and the builder of the first store was Mr Jenkins. A town reserve was proclaimed in June of that year. Tambo has one of the oldest registered racing clubs in Queensland, the first recorded race meeting being held there in 1873. A hospital was opened that year, the Queensland National Bank in 1875 and a Post Office the following year,

PLATE 52

Arthur Street, Tambo, showing damage after rain, 1877

When a loaded wagon or cart moved off the gravelled strip in the middle of the road onto the wet black soil, the damage that it caused made conditions difficult for other road users. In this shot, the ground has now dried out but the wet weather damage in the foreground has not yet been repaired.

The rain would have been very welcome as drinking water was at a premium. During 1875, over 200,000 sheep and 50,000 cattle went through the Tambo run and watered at the main waterhole, so the water was extremely muddy. It was 1880 before the Government built a dam to supply drinking water to the townsfolk. In 1875, the township had a population of 83 people. By comparison, stock returns for the district for the year 1873 showed that there were 409 horses, 6,469 cattle, 69,400 sheep and 70 pigs.

Plate 53

Tambo State School, 1877

The first schoolmaster at Tambo, Mr Alfred Groom, is shown here with 34 of his pupils. Visits to western centres by travelling photographers were not common, so this would probably be the first time that these children had been photographed.

The Tambo School opened in February 1876, more than two years after the School Building Committee submitted an application to the Department of Public Instruction. Mr Groom commenced teaching with an attendance of 26 pupils. His annual salary was £250.6.0. For the first few months, water to supply the school was carried in casks from a waterhole until the Department supplied the iron tank that can be seen on the left of the photo. The school ground was not fenced and the black soil became very muddy in wet weather. There were no trees on the site, and the area was exposed to the cold winter southerlies and the hot summer winds.

PLATE 54

Shamrock Street, Blackall, 1877

A flag flies high over the almost deserted main street of Blackall, which, like Tambo, lies on the banks of the Barcoo River. There has been a recent shower as evidenced by the wheel tracks gouged into the black soil road.

Major Thomas Mitchell was the first European to explore the Blackall district on his 1846 expedition into western Queensland. The tall waving Mitchell grass he encountered was named after him. The township was named in 1868 after Queensland's second governor, Sir Samuel Blackall. The district became an important wool-growing area and the legendary Jack Howe, who shore a record 321 sheep in 7 hours 40 minutes with hand shears lived and died there. Today Blackall has the last intact example of a steam-powered wool washing plant (wool scour) in Australia.

Plate 55

The washpool at Bowen Downs, known as the Pool of Siloam, 1877

In the early days, each sheep station had a washpool, formed by damming a creek. The sheep were washed before shearing because of the high cost of freight and shipping and because the price for greasy wool was lower than for washed wool. The sheep were pushed into a gidyea-lined trench filled with water from the washpool and soaked at 70°F for ten minutes. A sheep-washer then scrubbed them on a roller under jets of water, known as 'the spouts'. It took about half a minute to wash a sheep and the average number completed per hour was 50 to 70. The sheep then climbed up a race to stoned draining yards. The industry later changed from washing the sheep before shearing to scouring the wool after shearing.

Bowen Downs, taken up in 1861, was a huge property extending about 240 kilometres from north of the present towns of Aramac and Muttaburra to south of the present town of Longreach. Nat Buchanan drove the first mob of 5,000 cattle from Landsborough's Fort Cooper Station, near Nebo to Bowen Downs late in 1862. John Rule and Dyson Lacy introduced sheep to the district in 1863. Part of Bowen Downs was severed in 1872 and became Mt Cornish, after Henry Redford (immortalised in Rolf Boldrewood's 'Robbery Under Arms') drove 1000 stolen cattle across unoccupied country towards Adelaide and disposed of them in South Australia.

Taylor, CRD p16; Hogan, BQH p108; Pike, QF p119

Plate 56

Aramac station homestead, 1877

This substantial homestead was constructed before 1877. As with all his photographs, John Mills recorded the location in his own handwriting.

John Rule and Dyson Lacy were the first to occupy the Aramac Pastoral holding in May 1863. The property changed hands in 1872 when Roderick Travers purchased it. He had extensive pastoral interests in the Clermont district and considered that this country was better than the Peak Downs for sheep raising, with Aramac Creek having permanent water equal to that of the Barcoo River.

Plate 57

Wool teams at Aramac, 1877

This photograph shows wool teams from Bowen Downs on their way to the coast for shipment overseas. They travelled at about two kilometres per hour and combined with wet weather delays the journey could take many months.

Aramac had its beginnings when John Kingston, who had emigrated from England in 1864, gave up sheep herding on Aramac Station in 1867 to start up his Wayside hotel beside a large waterhole on Aramac Creek. The teamsters who brought stores from Clermont had been making good use of this area as a temporary rest camp for their animals. The area consisted of wide-open pastoral land covered with Mitchell grass and shaded by boree trees. In 1869, the Aramac town reserve was declared and in that year James Thomas Tilbury travelled from Rockhampton to Aramac where he established the first known grocer and draper's store in the area. A thriving township soon developed.

Kingston, A-PH p6-7

Plate 58

Dr Ben Poulton's residence, 1877

Dr Poulton was Aramac's first general practitioner, starting his practice in 1876. He soon became the secretary of Aramac's first school. He was still practising early in 1877 when Reckitt & Mills visited, but was replaced by Dr Spark soon afterwards. The first hospital was built and opened in 1879, with Dr Murdoch Matheson in charge.

This photograph has appeared in another publication labelled 'Aramac's first police station 1872'. It is possible that the building did have this earlier use, but this photo was taken by John Mills in 1877 and they labelled it 'Dr Ben Poulton's residence'. Magnification of the brass plate on the gate confirms this information.

Plate 59

Grey Rock Hotel on the Clermont-Aramac Road, 1877

The hotel on the left of this photo was situated 38 kilometres east of Aramac. Wayside shanties like this were located at regular intervals along Queensland's dray roads so that weary travellers could remove the dust, find refreshment and have somewhere to camp for the night. They also became 'stages' for the Cobb & Co. coaches where these operated. In the late 1870s, a Cobb & Co. coach travelled once a week from Clermont to Aramac, stopping overnight at the Surbiton Hotel, 105 km west of Clermont, and at Springer's Hotel on the Alice River. On the return journey, it made overnight stops at Grey Rock Hotel, Mr Doonan's hotel at Lagoon Creek and at Red Rock Hotel.

This road lost its importance when the railway line being constructed westwards from Rockhampton reached the north-south road between Blackall and Aramac. The town of Barcaldine was established at this junction. The road beside the railway, now known as the Capricorn Highway, superseded the Clermont-Aramac Road, which remains today as a series of tracks linking station properties. The need for the Grey Rock Hotel disappeared and it faded into oblivion.

O'Donnell, HCD p145

Plate 60

Alice River Aboriginals, 1877

The wagon route that linked Aramac to Clermont crossed the Alice River about 60 kilometres east of Aramac. When Reckitt & Mills travelled this way, some members of the local Aboriginal tribe were camped near the crossing. They seemed quite happy to pose for this photograph, which they would have been able to inspect soon after it was taken, as all photographs had to be developed in the photographers' mobile darkroom without delay.

The partners took many photographs of Aboriginals, in groups like this and as studio portraits.

Plate 61

Springsure, 1877

This view shows the township of Springsure fourteen years after A.C. Gregory first surveyed it. The first Post Office was established in 1864 and following year the Queensland Pastoral Society held Queensland's first Pastoral Show at Springsure. The first hospital, built of locally made bricks, was completed in 1868 and is still in existence. A state school opened two years later.

In December 1844, Ludwig Leichhardt was the first European to visit the Springsure area, with settlers gradually following, bringing sheep and some cattle. A settlement developed at this location because it lay on the wagon route leading from Rockhampton to the Gulf country and the Barcoo, and permanent springs in Springsure Creek provided water for the horse and bullock teams. The town derived its name from these springs.

Johnston & Campbell, B-OHYLG pp7-10

Plate 62

Springsure station homestead, with its owner Mr W.H. Richards at the gate, 1877

In 1859, tenders were called for four holdings situated roughly at the four points of the compass around Springsure. Springsure station was one of them and Geo. Ranken Jnr took it up in 1861. W.H. Richards acquired it soon afterwards. The stations in the district thrived during the 1870s, and Springsure station supported 56 residents.

During 1860 and 1861, tension between the Aboriginals and Europeans in this area had mounted, with the Aboriginals killing a number of individuals and stock, and the Native Mounted Police, urged on by squatters, 'dispersing' and exterminating the local groups. This culminated in the Wills Massacre at Cullin-la-ringo, 30 kilometres northwest of Springsure, in 1861. It was the worst white massacre in the history of Australian settlement, with nineteen men, women and children losing their lives. Native police and squatters then hunted Aboriginals for days, killing many.

Johnston & Campbell, B-OHYLG pp5,14

PLATE 63

Clermont in its original location beside Diggings Lagoon, Sandy Creek, late 1870s

This was a beautiful setting for a town, which probably explains the reason for the choice of site. It turned out to be a disastrous decision as the buildings were erected on the low-lying northern bank of the creek in what was a rather obvious flood plain. The bridge across the creek links the township with the higher bank, which is above flood level.

Payable gold was discovered in Nelson's Gully, a tributary of Sandy Creek, in 1861 and by the end of the following year 1,000 miners were working in the district. The firm of Winter & Lea (initially Winter & Veale) first established a general store at this site in 1862 and the Diggings Lagoon settlement became known as Winter & Veales before being surveyed and named Clermont late in 1863.

O'Donnell, HCD p21

PLATE 64

Drummond Street, Clermont, late 1870s

These buildings are located along the bank of the lagoon on the opposite side of the road to the Winter & Lea building. The saddler on the right is Robert A. Gaebel.

Local Aboriginals had warned the Europeans of the likelihood of flooding, but to no avail. The foolishness of building a township in a flood plain was to bring about the destruction of all this in 1917 when a devastating flood several metres deep swept through drowning 65 people. The town was then relocated to the opposite higher bank, with the surviving buildings being towed to their new position by a steam tractor. It is fortunate that photographers like Reckitt & Mills have recorded scenes like these so that some record of the original town is available today.

Plate 65

A steam traction engine in operation, late 1800s

A road locomotive like this had tremendous low-speed power and could easily take the place of a large bullock team.

There is no real reason why the use of steam engines on roads should not have enjoyed a success equal to that of the railway engine, but its development was limited by the unsuitability of most roads, the jealousy of other road users, and the time that it took to fire up. It did achieve general utility for heavy traction work and other duties such as road rolling, and could be readily adapted from road haulage to power farm machines. It was a distinguished product of nineteenth-century steam technology but the internal combustion engine superseded it in the early 1900s.

Plate 66

Peak Downs copper mine, Copperfield, late 1870s

The township of Copperfield was in its death throes when this photo was taken. The huge smelters visible in the distance were about to close down, and with no source of employment the town would soon disappear from the map.

A huge outcrop of almost pure copper was discovered in 1861, about 8 kilometres southwest of Clermont. The town of some 2,000 people that sprang up was named Coppperfield. Development peaked in about 1867 when the smelters worked day and night and the town was a hive of activity. The population then began to decline and the company was eventually wound up in 1877. The last ore was smelted in 1879. The numbers had dropped to about 900 in 1879 and 400 in 1881, with many of the departing population moving to Clermont. Thomas Butcher Ricketts and his wife and children were among those who made this move. One of the daughters would later become the wife of John Mills.

Plate 67

A bullock team hauls a loaded wagon across the Isaacs River, late 1870s

While one bullock team struggles to haul its load up the bank out of the water, a second team that has already negotiated the crossing waits on the high bank at the top left of the photo. Teams usually travelled in pairs so that they could be double banked on steep sections. The site of this crossing is on the present Peak Downs Highway near the town of Moranbah.

During the annual wet seasons, boggy conditions and numerous flooded creeks and rivers cut Queensland's dray roads for long periods. This crossing on the Clermont-Nebo road was one location where long delays occurred. If they were unable to cross, the bullock drivers would make camp and wait until the water receded.

Plate 74

Fossicking at Mount Britton, 1881

Payable gold was discovered at the Mount Britton diggings on the Nebo Gold Field inland from Mackay in February 1881. A rush soon followed. Life for a miner involved hard physical labour, but the lure of gold and the hope of making a fortune kept the fossickers working tirelessly. This is one of scores of photographs taken by Reckitt & Mills on the Nebo Gold Field in the 1880s. It shows a group of fossickers panning for alluvial gold in Oaky Creek. Gold pans, large shallow tin dishes, are being used to separate the lighter materials from the heavy particles of gold.

Reckitt & Mills soon became gold miners themselves and as the population decreased, they spent more time on that activity than they did taking photographs.

Ford, BTM p83

Plate 75

Sluicing at William Orange's claim, Mount Britton, 1881

One of the first prospectors was Billy Orange, whose original claim was jumped by a party of four men from the nearby township of Nebo. When the Mining Warden arrived from Clermont in April, he awarded Orange another claim and this photograph shows him hard at work sluicing wash dirt. Water was essential for the separation of the fine alluvial gold from the sand and gravel, so the diggers often built sluices to bring water from a dam or spring to the mining claim. The sluice in the background of this photo has been made from bark. Alluvium was shovelled into the water flow at the end of the sluice and the gold was caught in the riffles or cross strips as the wash dirt was swept down the slope.

The Government of the day had great difficulty deciding who should receive the reward for having discovered payable gold at Mount Britton. There were four claimants – James Heenan, Billy Orange, Ward and Thompson McFadzen. It took two years of investigation before a ruling was finally made in favour of Orange. He used his reward money to buy a horse team and moved to Croydon and the Gulf country, returning to the Nebo district, poorer but wiser, 18 months later.

Ford, BTM pp73-4

PLATE 76

Cradling at Mount Britton, 1881

Here an 'American cradle' (or box sluice) is being used to separate the gold from the wash dirt. Rocking the cradle from side to side separates the gold and is more productive than panning with a dish. One man is handling the alluvium and placing it into the cradle. Another is rocking the cradle and using a dipper to throw water into the head of the sluice, while a third uses a pan to winnow the gold from the other heavier elements left behind at the bottom of the cradle. The fourth man on the left is excavating the wash dirt.

As soon as the gold rush began, enterprising men in Mackay and Walkerston began making cradles and selling them to the diggers on the field.

Ford, BTM p84

Plate 77

Eb Gibson's butchery, Mount Britton, 1881-82

Ebenezer Gibson was a bachelor when he set up his butcher shop and store early in the gold rush using a few sheets of bark and saplings. The first beast that he killed was cut up and sold off the gallows as the meat-hungry diggers rushed the yard. Eb and his assistant simply cut pieces of beef off the carcase and handed it out. The price was 4d per lb cash. Those who did not have cash paid with grains of gold, the weight being guessed. When Harold Finch-Hatton arrived on the field soon afterwards, Eb's butchery was the only building that had any appearance of permanence about it. Plenty of beef was available as he was running in two or three cattle a week from the nearby property of Homevale and killing them in a sapling yard near the shop.

He soon built this more substantial building. Timber was in plentiful supply so saplings were bolted, nailed or wired together to provide a framework. Bark was stripped from large trees and flattened to provide cladding for the roof and walls, while other saplings on the outside held the bark in place.

Ford, BTM pp69,166

Plate 78

Royal Mail Hotel, Mount Britton, 1881-82

Henry Steinman built this hotel early in the rush. A group of thirsty patrons have gathered outside to pose for this photo. They were able to squander their money here at any time of the day or night. A lamp was hanging above the front entrance to facilitate the entry and exit of those who liked to drink into the night. This was the second hotel to open on the field, the first being the Diggers' Arms built by Dan Nolan.

The number of diggers on the Mount Britton field during 1881 quickly rose to 1500 and hotels and stores flourished. The first licensing board hearing early in May adjourned the applications for a fortnight pending the erection of buildings. Six licences were subsequently issued during July. These went to Dan Nolan, Henry Steinman, William Landells, Charles Ferris, Michael Brolly and Alexander Louis Smith. The Royal Mail closed in 1884 after the rush had subsided but the Diggers' Arms and its successor, the Mount Britten Hotel (sic), remained open until 1902.

Ford, BTM p78

Plate 79

The Mackay Hotel, Mount Britton, 1881-82

William Landells, who had been the proprietor of the Ship Inn in Sydney Street, Mackay, opened this hotel on the southern approach to the township early in the rush. This photograph was taken late in 1881 or early in 1882 when Landells decided to sell out. The impending closure is confirmed by the 'Duffered Out' sign, which in mining terminology signifies that a claim has been worked out. A close examination reveals that an Aboriginal family is included among the patrons. It is apparent that Landells built the right-hand half of the building first, and added an extension later using galvanised iron for the roof. He operated a general store in conjunction with the hotel, as did many other hotelkeepers in small settlements. The sign above the door on the left hand side of the building reads, 'W. LANDELLS, MACKAY HOTEL, MT. BRITTON'. James O'Toole took over the business from Landells and operated it until the end of 1887.

Landells was one of Mackay's first settlers, having arrived on the ship *Murray* in February 1863, a week after Port Mackay was first declared a 'port of entry and clearance'.

Ford, BTM p79

Plate 80

The Leo Hotel and Diggers' Rest, Mount Britton, 1881-82

This hotel, opened by Charles Ferris, was one of the six establishments that started up early in the rush. The Hon. Harold Finch-Hatton was the only 'Magistrate of the Territory' (Justice of the Peace) on the field at that time. When he first arrived, he pitched his tent at the site of what was to become the Mount Britton township, but soon found that he had two stores, the post office, the tobacconist and bookseller's shop and five public houses (including this one) surrounding his abode. He describes what happened next as follows:

> One of these infernal public houses was put up a few yards from my tent, and sleep at night became out of the question.
>
> An army of drunken revellers made night hideous with their yells. They used to start drinking about sundown, and pass successively through the convivial, uproarious, and quarrelsome stages of drunkenness during the night, ending with total collapse about five in the morning. No early-closing interfered with the even tenor of their enjoyment, and there were no police to damp the geniality of their proceedings … Nearly every night one or more of these Bacchanalians would stagger into my tent, and either collapse in a shapeless heap on the floor or begin shouting for liquor in language that made the whole place smell of sulphur.

Little wonder that Finch-Hatton decided to shift his camp upstream to a location not far from the reefs, where he built a humpy of box-tree bark.

Ford, BTM p80

PLATE 81

The Doctor's residence, Mount Britton, 1881-82

This building was erected next to the Royal Mail Hotel by Dr C.O. Handt. He was a middle-aged German doctor, who was not accredited in Australia because of his homeopathic qualifications, but was on the field for over a year and provided an invaluable service to the diggers during that time. Many of them took advantage of his good nature and did not pay him for his services. Harold Finch-Hatton tried to assist by insisting that all of the workers in his mines paid for any services rendered.

The doctor had a prospecting claim of his own that he worked at his leisure, but once when he had to go to Nebo in connection with an inquest, three Italian scoundrels jumped his claim. This distressed him greatly and he remonstrated with them at length while they ignored him and proceeded to work his claim. The newly arrived police constable was not prepared to intervene and the Mining Warden, whose duty it was to resolve such disputes, was two days' ride away in Clermont.

Ford, BTM p80

PLATE 82

Reckitt & Mills photographic studio, Mount Britton, 1881-2

At the beginning of the Mount Britton rush, John Mills and Albert Reckitt built this photographic studio near the bank of Oaky Creek where a large fig tree now stands. Like all the early buildings, it was constructed of saplings and bark. The nameplate above the door reads, 'Queensland Photo Company, Reckitt and Mills'.

When the Reverend Albert Alexander MacLaren visited the field in May 1882, the partners made the studio available for a church service on the Monday evening. A very attentive congregation filled the building. After the service was over, a meeting was held for the purpose of taking steps to acquire a provisional school on the diggings. A subscription list was drawn up and about £25 subscribed towards the purchase of a suitable building, the idea being that this would become a Public Hall and also be suitable for use as a school until such time as the Department of Public Instruction provided its own school building. The attendees appointed a committee to arrange for the erection and management of the Public Hall and John Mills took on the position of 'Secretary and Treasurer'. On the next evening, a very pleasant couple of hours was spent in the same room, when songs, readings and recitations were given. Rev. MacLaren was impressed. He afterwards wrote, 'The diggers have some very good comic singers amongst their number.'

Ford, BTM pp82,94

Plate 83

The Mills family cottages, Mount Britton, ca 1883

When Mills married Mary Ann Louisa Ricketts in October 1882, he converted the photographic studio into accommodation, partitioning off a bedroom at the front and building an enormous fireplace at the rear. Behind this building, he built a separate bathhouse. Near the back of the block, there was a humpy for his partner, Albert Reckitt, with a buggy shed behind that. The other sapling and bark building to the left was constructed later. It became the bedroom and living room, and the original bedroom was converted to a storeroom. This second building had a scullery behind it and another large fireplace for cooking behind that.

Mills drew a plan of the site, which shows the layout of the improvements. There was a large bee shed in the middle of the block behind the cottages and, later on, two more bee sheds and a fowl house at the rear near a stone heap and waterhole. Flowerbeds and vegetable gardens, with pathways between them, occupied the remainder of the block.

Ford, BTM p101

PLATE 84

The Pubic Hall/School of Arts, ca 1883

After a public meeting in May 1882, that elicited support for the provision of a Public Hall, work proceeded on its construction and this building was completed a few months later. It consisted of a hardwood frame, covered with bark and galvanised iron, and it had hardwood floorboards. The internal dimensions were 41 feet x 16 feet. As it had no internal lining, it became very hot inside during the day.

In October, a raised platform was added to provide a stage. It also acted as a pulpit for the pastor when he visited. From that time on, the building became the 'School of Arts' as well as the 'Public Hall' and it became the venue for amateur concerts. These functions raised funds for the maintenance and upkeep of the hall. The Mount Britton correspondent in the *Mackay Mercury* said that 'the institution is well supported by the public and may be said to be in a flourishing condition, and solvent, thanks to our Treasurer and Secretary, Mr. J.H. Mills, for the interest he takes in the concern.'

Ford, BTM p97

Plate 85

Mount Britton township, 1883

By the end of 1883, a number of bark and sapling buildings had been built on 'the flat' on the eastern bank of Oaky Creek. This photograph shows the Public Hall on the left. The building third from the left is the Reckitt & Mills photographic studio. On the right a corner of the Mount Britton Hotel can be seen and the next building along from it is the Leo Hotel and Diggers' Rest. The buildings are lined up on either side of what was to become Stevenson Street, named after the local Member of Parliament.

Ford, BTM p76

PLATE 86

The first courthouse, Mount Britton, 1883

The Government invited tenders for the erection of a Courthouse/Police Station in February 1883 but construction had not commenced when the newly appointed Police Magistrate, Mineral Lands Commissioner and Mining Warden arrived in town. Accordingly, this bark and sapling humpy became a temporary Courthouse. Mr J. Vivian Williams was the new appointee on transfer from Maryborough. The Maryborough News had this to say about his appointment:

> He has been long and favourable known in Maryborough, and we are certain the inhabitants of Mount Britton will have great reason to congratulate themselves upon the appointment. That gentleman is of a quiet and discriminating turn of mind, well versed in law, not easily perturbed, and generally inclined to take a fair and impartial view of whatever may be brought before him for judicial consideration.

Ford, BTM p107

Plate 87

The new Courthouse/Police Station, Mount Britton, 1884

This new combined Courthouse/Police Station was officially opened in July 1884, fifteen months after Mr J. Vivian Williams arrived in town and three years after the first Police presence was established in the area. Mr Williams was considered to be a very good Warden and Police Magistrate and considerably enhanced his reputation when he gave a grand ball to celebrate the opening. About 50 people attended and dancing continued until an early hour the next morning. On the following night, entertainment was provided for the youngsters and the school children were presented with prizes. During 1885, however, Mr Williams was withdrawn from the field. Senior Constable John Bradley became the Mining Registrar and Senior Constable R. Woodhouse the acting Clerk of Petty Sessions.

By 1887, white ants had badly damaged the building so the Police vacated it and moved into the former Post and Telegraph Office. It seems that the building remained vacant until November 1892, when Albert Reckitt bought it by Public Auction. The Mills family moved in a couple of years later and named it 'Cairnedie'.

Ford, BTM pp116,117,120-121,137

Plate 88

Mount Britton township from the west, late 1880s

Gradually, substantial timber buildings with galvanized roofs replaced the original bark and sapling humpies. This photograph shows the scene from the hill on the opposite side of Oaky Creek in the late1880s. Stevenson Street runs from left to right, with the Courthouse/ Police Station visible at the northern end on the left and the Post and Telegraph office at the southern end on the right. The Public Hall/School of Arts is located across the main road from the P&T Office in the right foreground. The second building from the left is the Diggers' Arms Hotel and the buildings in the middle foreground comprise Eb Gibson's butchery.

Ford, BTM p119

Plate 89

Top and bottom tunnels *Forge* *Main shaft*

The Little Wanderer Prospecting Claim, Mount Britton, 1880s

Most of the early prospectors were interested only in the easy pickings of alluvial mining but a few concentrated on searching for reefs. Charles Gibbard was the first to find a reef and named it the Little Wanderer. The Hon. Harold Finch-Hatton, with his partners John and Dick Absolon, located the Erratic Star soon afterwards and then bought a controlling interest in the Little Wanderer.

In July 1881, Finch-Hatton travelled south to order crushing machinery and in June the following year, after many difficulties, he commissioned the Sabbath Calm battery. Six weeks later a shipment of over 1000 ounces of gold arrived at the A.J.S. Bank in Mackay. In October, Finch-Hatton travelled to Melbourne where he launched the Mount Britten (sic) Gold Mining Company to take over his mines and the battery.

Ford, BTM pp86-7

PLATE 90

The Edith Mary Prospecting Claim, Mount Britton, ca 1900

This photograph shows John Mills on the left and his son Bert (Albert Mount Britton Mills) working on the Mills family's claim.

Soon after Reckitt & Mills set up their photographic studio in 1881, they began prospecting for reefs. A promising quartz seam was located one mile west of the township and they began putting down a shaft. They named the claim after Albert Reckitt's daughter, Edith Mary, who was only two years old when he took her back to his sisters in England after his wife died in 1866. By the end of 1883, one shaft was down 40 feet and another down 100 feet, with some excellent specimens having been obtained. The best return ever netted from the Edith Mary was £260 in a fortnight. In 1886, the partners entered some specimens in the Colonial and Indian Exhibition at South Kensington in England and were delighted to receive a medal and a magnificent certificate.

Ford, BTM p145

Plate 91

Beekeeping at Mount Britton, 1890s

From a few hives in a shelter at the back of their first cottage, John Mills built up his apiary to over 60 hives, housed in three sheds. The original cottage was dismantled to provide the materials.

'Mills Honey' became well known throughout the Mackay district and during the 1890s, beekeeping became the main source of income for the family. This industry enabled them to remain at Mount Britton long after other families had left. In February 1898, Cyclone Eline caused considerable damage to the sheds and many of the hives, but most of them recovered. Occasionally Mills travelled to Nebo to collect supplies, fulfil orders for honey, seek new orders and collect outstanding debts. After the cyclone, the road to Nebo was not fit to travel by buggy for several weeks, and it was Friday 1 April before he made the first trip that year.

Ford, BTM p150

Plate 92

Cairnedie, Mount Britton, ca 1896

The Mills family moved into their new home in the old Courthouse/Police Station in about 1895. John had earlier fenced the site to keep the goats out and the pets in. They then set about developing the site, planting extensive flower and vegetable gardens.

Albert Reckitt took this photograph showing John and his son Bert hard at work.

Ford, BTM p143

Plate 93

Back row: Ethel Mills 14, …, Mabel Nolan 17, Daisy Richards 15, …, Lily Richards 13, Mr Arthur Wilson
Middle row: …, …, John Henry Burgess 12 or Bill Burgess 9, …, Edie Mills 12, …
Front row: …, Cyril Mills 9, Leslie Richards 11, Flora Mills 4

Mount Britton Provisional School, 1902

The teacher in this photograph, Arthur Wilson, arrived in July 1899 from Golden Gate School near Croydon. He left for Plane Creek School near Sarina in September 1902, soon after John Mills took this photograph. The photo includes at least one pupil who had already finished her schooling (Mabel) and one who had not yet started (Flora).

The Mount Britton Provisional School opened in the Public Hall during 1883 and a succession of teachers officiated, with gaps of 18 months on two occasions. The school committee dismantled the hall at the end of 1894 and used the materials to construct a smaller school on the nearby School Reserve. When the school closed permanently in 1906, Edie Mills took on the responsibility of teaching the younger children until the Mills family moved to Mackay in 1908.

Ford, BTM p173

Plate 94

An outing in the buggy, ca 1903

Here the Mills family members are dressed in their Sunday best and appear to be heading off on a Sunday afternoon outing, probably to visit the Richards family at the nearby property of Homevale. Cyril, Maud, Mary, Edie and Flora Mills are in the buggy while Ethel is standing in front.

Ford, BTM p176

Plate 95

Albert Reckitt's headstone, Mount Britton, 1905

This is the headstone on Albert Reckitt's grave, provided by John Mills soon after Albert's burial. Mills also arranged for the area to be fenced as a family graveyard.

Albert's death was a tragedy for the Mills household. He fell ill with a fever in the second week of March 1905 and his condition deteriorated rapidly. He did not respond to treatment and passed away on 24 March aged 75 years. All members of the Mills family were heartbroken. They buried him in the Mount Britton cemetery alongside baby Ernest. John read the burial service, as he had done on many previous occasions, and after the ceremony, he leaned against a tree and cried. It was the only time that the children ever saw their father in tears.

Ford, BTM p180

Plate 96

Mount Britton cemetery, 1905

The fence shown here around the Mills family graves is still in place today. Keith and Warren Mills, descendants of John, have added a plaque in memory of infant Ernest, who is buried alongside Albert Reckitt. Descendants of Bill and Eleanor Burgess have separately marked the grave of Susan Scandish, the mother of Eleanor.

Other unmarked graves at this cemetery include those of John Duff, Johann Michael Vogel, George Condon, Edward Jackson, William Ford, Eliza Maclean, an infant female Hobson and Sarah O'Toole.

Ford, BTM p180

Plate 97

Flora and Maud Mills in the billygoat cart, Mount Britton, ca 1902

The Mills family relied on goats for their dairy products, so a billygoat cart was an obvious attraction for the children. Their older brother Cyril also rode in it.

Flora used to relate that on occasions, Cyril would entice her on to the back of a goat and then mischievously twist its tail to make it buck her off.

Ford, BTM p181

Plate 98

A typical backyard scene at Cairnedie, Mount Britton, ca 1902

A close inspection of this photo showing the outhouse reveals Flora and Maud Mills playing in the shade of the choko vine with a home-made cart. The hardships that their parents suffered did not stop the children from enjoying life at Mount Britton.

The two girls also used to play in the old cell at the back of the house, still in place from the days when the building was a police station and courthouse.

Ford, BTM p182

Plate 99

The Treloar family in front of their slab house at Hampden, 30 kilometres north of Mackay, 1907

This house was built by Harry Treloar who arrived in Bowen from England in 1873. He married Kate Collins in 1883 and they settled here at Hampden. They had five children between 1883 and 1891. After Kate died in 1893, Lilla Parveez became the housekeeper and raised the children. She is shown with Flossie, Ivy (in front), Bert, Reg and Percy. Harry was a carpenter, who also built the original Hampden State School, which closed in 1918, and the first Kuttabul Hotel nearby.

Slab houses were a popular form of construction in pioneering times. Some builders used vertical slabs but this horizontal style was more popular. Grooved corner and intermediate posts were set in the ground or on a horizontal base plate and the slabs were inserted from above, one on top of another. Unfortunately, shrinkage caused gaps to appear between the slabs, which was an advantage in summer but less than ideal in winter.

Archer, GAD p68

Plate 100

The Waters family, Finch Hatton, 1907

'Old Dave' Waters and his wife are shown here in front of their house ready for an outing in the buggy. A younger couple has joined them and their adopted daughter May is holding the horse. They are all dressed in their Sunday best.

Dave had owned a hotel at Finch Hatton before acquiring this small farm at Netherdale, a few kilometres to the west.

Plate 101

The Jordan family beside their house at Hampden, north of Mackay, 1907

This is a typical farmer's cottage on timber stumps with the usual veranda. The side wall has been faced with corrugated iron. Banana trees are growing alongside the house and other trees surround it. The owners, Mary and Harry Jordan, have lined up with their children, from left to right, Edith, Sophia, Robert, Percy and Henry. Four older children, Jane, Grace, Fred and Charlotte would have left home by the time this photo was taken. Henry later married Leila Hudson, a distant relative of the author.

Soon after they married in 1880, Harry and Mary selected this property and built the house at what is now Mulei, near the junction of the Marian-Hampden Road and the Bruce Highway.

Plate 102

Alexander (Sandy) Watt's team at Benholme, between Mirani and Gargett, 1907

In the early days of the sugar industry in Queensland, the cane was cut and loaded by hand onto wagons and drawn to the mill or railway siding by horse teams. Here Sandy Watt, on the right, proudly shows off his team of six horses with their load of Badilla cane ready for hauling to the Mirani West railway siding. The cane was much thicker and taller than it is today. The other man in the photo would be Mick Ready.

Sandy and his wife Emma had their first three children, Alexander James, Herbert and Lucy at Tamborine, south-east of Brisbane. They then moved to Benholme, 40 kilometres west of Mackay, in 1892 where they had three more children, Ivy, May and Roy. The difference in age between Alex and Roy was twenty years.

Plate 103

The loco at North Eton sugar mill, south west of Mackay, 1907

Sugar mills throughout Queensland used tramlines, now known as cane railways, to bring the cane to the mill for crushing. Some early mills used a gauge of 3 feet 6 inches but eventually a gauge of 2 feet became standard. This photo shows the North Eton steam locomotive, known colloquially as a 'loco', hauling a load of cane to the mill.

The North Eton mill began crushing in 1888 but did not install a tramline until 1895 when the Double Peak Central Tramway Company Limited was registered. Ten miles of permanent line and five miles of portable line were ordered, but the only locomotive available was smaller than the directors had planned. It was purchased and performed quite satisfactorily for many years.

Rolleston, TD p40

Plate 104

An outing on Sandy Creek at Beldan's property, North Eton, 1907

The Beldan family entertain their visitors with a Sunday afternoon outing on the north branch of Sandy Creek. The young men are dressed in suits and ties and the women and girls in their best dresses. Everyone is wearing a hat, so they were obviously aware of the need for protection from the sun.

Eli Beldan, who married Margaret Carson, took up this property on Noel Lamb's road in the 1880s. They started with cattle, later growing sugar cane. Their children were Thomas James (Sonny), Annie (Nancy), Edmond, Grace, John (Jack) and Herbert (Bert). Eli was the Chairman of Directors at North Eton mill at the time.

Plate 105

Back row: Nell Culverhouse, George Hudson holding Henry, Lizzie Hudson, Mary Ann Louisa Mills, John and Elsie Williams, Clem Culverhouse holding Tally
Middle row: Frances Williams, John Henry Williams, Harry Williams, Stanley and Ethel Williams, Leila Williams, Edie Mills, Hetty Williams
Front row: Flora and Maud Mills, Leila Hudson, Maurice and Dafydd Williams, Ethel, Rita and Stanley Culverhouse, Bert Williams
Absent: Bert Mills

The wedding of Stanley Williams and Ethel Mills, Mackay, 17 June 1908

The number of people in this family photograph was huge as Stanley had nine brothers and sisters (one of whom was already married with four children) and the bride had five brothers and sisters. Not surprisingly, the bride's father is not in the picture as he was fully occupied behind the camera.

It was this impending marriage of his eldest daughter that finally convinced Mills to relocate the family from Mount Britton to Mackay early in 1908.

Ford, BTM p192

Plate 106

Holy Trinity Church, Alfred Street, Mackay, after the 1918 cyclone

Dozens of buildings were flattened or seriously damaged by the cyclone that hit Mackay on the night of Sunday 20 January. Flora Mills played the organ at the church service that night as the wind began to howl outside and the rain came down in torrents. Little did she realise that the building would look like this the next morning. The Rector, Canon James Norman, and the Reverend I. Butterworth watched the destruction from the back of the Rectory after first seeing half of the Sunday School blown over the top of the Rectory into Wood Street, where it blocked traffic for a fortnight.

The cyclone arrived without warning, and wind gusts of over 200 kph tore through the district. The barometer dropped to 27.55 inches (933 mbs), which is the lowest reading ever recorded in Queensland. It was slightly worse than Cyclone Tracy, which hit Darwin in 1974.

Ford, BTM pp197-98

Plate 107

Damage to the Sydney Street Bridge caused by the tidal surge that followed the cyclone, Mackay, 1918.

A tidal surge travelled across the town as far as Nebo Road and a number of spans of the bridge were destroyed when the *Brinawarr* crashed into it. It was one of the tenders that ferried passengers and cargo between the town wharves and the coastal steamers anchored at Flat Top.

Over 1.4 metres of rain fell in the five-day period. Artie Fadden (later Sir Arthur Fadden) was Town Clerk at the time and became secretary of the emergency committee that organised the town and rationed available food supplies.

Ford, BTM p197

PLATE 108

The Grand Hotel after the cyclone, Mackay, 1918

The tidal surge deposited a large buoy from the Flat Top Island anchorage in front of this hotel on the corner of Victoria and Brisbane Streets, over two kilometres from the sea.

Because of the bad weather, it was the third night after the tragedy before anyone was able to notify the outside world about what had happened. After unsuccessful attempts on the previous two nights, a young lad, Jack Vidulich, was able to signal details of the disaster from the upper floor of this hotel to George Rendall, the supervisor of the Flat Top Island lighthouse, using a Ford headlight to send Morse code. Rendall relayed the message to the *Wyreema*, which was standing by waiting for information. The historic message read, 'Cyclone, floods, tidal wave, loss of life, 14 bodies recovered. All wharves and sugar stores have collapsed. *Relief*, *Quasha* and *Brinawarr* sunk. *Tay*, *Apa* and *Pelican* ashore. Mackay is on military rations and only 10-day food supply on hand. It was two weeks after the cyclone before vitally needed food supplies and building materials arrived by ship. It is a vastly different world today.

Ford, DTM p197

Plate 109

Drying the merchandise outside Beirne's store in Sydney Street, Mackay, after the 1918 cyclone

The buildings in this photograph do not appear to have suffered much damage but it is apparent that a considerable amount of water damage has occurred to the stock. Residents worked around the clock for days cleaning up the mess and repairing the damage.

John Mills was now 66 years of age and the photographs that he took of the cyclone damage were to be his last, as he died the following year. The thousands of photos that he took in his lifetime have made a significant contribution to our knowledge and appreciation of what life was like for our pioneers in the early days of Queensland.

Ford, BTM p199

Bibliography

Archer, John, *The Great Australian Dream: The History of the Australian House*, Angus & Robertson, Sydney, 1996.

Armstrong, G.O. *In Mitchell's Footsteps: A History of the Balonne Shire*, Brisbane, 1968.

Bolton, G.C. *A Thousand Miles Away: A History of North Queensland to 1920*, Australian National University Press, Canberra, 1972.

Byrne, Dianne, *A Travelling Photographer in Colonial Queensland*, John Oxley Library, Brisbane, 1994

Evans, Ian, *The Australian Home*, Flannel Flower Press, Glebe, 1983.

Feetham, Rt. Rev. J.O. and Rymer, Rev. W.V. *North Queensland Jubilee Book 1878 – 1928*, The Corporation of the Synod of the Diocese of North Queensland, Townsville, 1929.

Ford, Lyall, *Below These Mountains: The Adventures of John Henry Mills – Pioneer Photographer and Gold Miner*, Taipan Press, Cairns, 2001.

Ford, Lyall, *Poorhouse to Paradise: The Adventures of a Pioneering Family in a North Queensland Country Town*, Taipan Press, Cairns, 2001.

Hogan, Janet, *Building Queensland's Heritage: National Trust Queensland*, Richmond Hill Press Pty Ltd, Richmond, 1978.

Hogan, Janet, and Winkle, Evan, *Queensland Heritage Sketchbook: National Trust Queensland*, Weldon Publishing Pty Ltd, Willoughby, 1988.

Holthouse, Hector, *Illustrated History of Queensland*, Rigby Limited, Brisbane, 1978.

Holthouse, Hector, *River of Gold*, Angus and Robertson, Sydney, 1967.

Johnston, W.R. and Campbell, B. *Bauhinia: One Hundred Years of Local Government*, Bauhinia Shire Council Centenary Committee, Springsure, 1979.

Kerr, John, *Pioneer Pageant*, Pioneer Shire Council, Mackay, 1980.

Kingston, Len, *Aramac 1870 – 1984: A Pictorial History*, self-published, Bundaberg, 1984.

Logan, Greg, and Watson, Tom, *Soldiers of the Service: Some Early Queensland Educators and Their Schools*, History of Queensland Education Society, Brisbane, 1992.

Mayes, George A. *Behold Nebo: a History of the Nebo Shire*, R & R Publications, Glenden, 1991.

Nolan, Carolyn, *River Country: The History of the Balonne Shire*, Balonne Shire Council, St George, 2003.

O'Donnell, Dan, *Belyando Shire: A History of Clermont and District*, Belyando Shire Council, Clermont, 1989.

Pike, Glenville, *Queensland Frontier*, Rigby Limited, Brisbane, 1978.

Rolleston, Frank, *The Defiance: The Story of North Eton Co-operative Sugar Milling Association Limited 1888* – 1987, North Eton Sugar Milling Association Limited, North Eton, 1987.

Springer, Elena, V. (ed), *Charters Towers Centenary 1872 – 1972*, City of Charters Towers, 1972.

Taylor, R.B. *Concerning Roma and District 1846 – 1885*, Volume 1, unpublished, Roma.